Geology Rocks!

Igneous Rock

Rebecca Faulkner

Raintree

Chicago, Illinois

Produced for Raintree Publishers by Discovery
Books Ltd
Editorial: Kathryn Walker, Melanie Waldron, and
Rachel Howells
Design: Vctoria Bevan, Rob Norridge,
and AMR Design Ltd (www.amrdesign.com)
Illustrations: David Woodroffe
Picture Research: Melissa Allison and Mica Brancic
Production: Duncan Gilbert
Originated by Chroma Graphics Pte. Ltd
Printed and bound in China by
South China Printing Company

12 11 10
10 9 8 7 6 5 4 3

**Library of Congress Cataloging-in-Publication
Data**
Faulkner, Rebecca.
    Igneous Rock / Rebecca Faulkner.
        p. cm. -- (Geology Rocks)
    Includes bibliographical references and index.
    ISBN-13: 978-1-4109-2771-2 (lib. bdg.)
    ISBN-10: 1-4109-2771-7 (lib. bdg.)
    ISBN-13: 978-1-4109-2779-8 (pbk.)
    ISBN-10: 1-4109-2779-2 (pbk.)
    1. Igneous Rock--Juvenile literature. I. Title.
    QE461.F354 2008
    552′1--dc22
                                2006037174

This leveled text is a version of *Freestyle:
Geology Rocks: Igneous Rock*.

Acknowledgments
The publishers would like to thank the following for
permission to reproduce photographs:

©Alamy p. **20** (Arco Images), p. **37** (Belinda Lawley),
p. **38** (Bernd Mellman), p. **23** (Dianna Bonner
Martin), p. **22** (GC Minerals), pp. **5 top inset, 30**
(LeighSmithImages), p. **41** (Photo Resource Hawaii);
©Collections pp. **5 bottom inset, 28** (Colin Inch);
©Corbis p. **11**, p. **42** (Alberto Garcia), p. **10** (Ashley
Cooper), p. **39 bottom** (Bettmann), p. **16** (David
Muench), p. **12** (Douglas Peebles), p. **32** (Galen
Rowell), p. **4** (Jeff Vanuga), p. **5** (Jim Sugar), pp. **24,
44** (Pablo Corral Vega), p. **35** (zefa/Tony Craddock);
©GeoScience Features Picture Library pp. **17, 18,
18-19 middle, 33**, p. **19** (Prof. B. Booth); ©Getty
Images p. **43**, (AFP Photo/Edgar Romero), p. **31**
(George Diebold), p. **6** (Iconica/Frans Lemmens),
p. **35 inset** (National Geographic/Paul Chelsey),
p. **26** (Photodisc), p. **15** (Photonica), p. **39 top**
(Riser), pp. **5 middle inset, 29** (Stone), p. **19**
(Visuals Unlimited); ©istockphoto.com p. **13**
(Maciej Laska), p. **13 inset** (Ralph Paprzycki); Nasa
p. **40**, p. **9** (Visible Earth); ©Photolibrary p. **25**;
©Science Photo Library p. **27** (Dirk Wiersma)

Cover photograph of Giant's Causeway in
County Antrim, Northern Ireland reproduced
with permission of ©Science Photo Library
(Lawrence Lawry).

Every effort has been made to contact copyright
holders of any material reproduced in this book.
Any omissions will be rectified in subsequent
printings if notice is given to the publishers.

Disclaimer
All the Internet addresses (URLs) given in this book
were valid at the time of going to press. However,
due to the dynamic nature of the Internet, some
addresses may have changed, or sites may have
changed or ceased to exist since publication. While
the author and publishers regret any inconvenience
this may cause readers, no responsibility for any
such changes can be accepted by either the author
or the publishers.

CONTENTS

Fiery Rocks 4

Crusty Old Rocks 6

Rocks Around the World 10

What Makes Igneous Rocks? 16

This Rock, That Rock 22

Buildings and Bling 28

Intrusions 32

Extrusions 36

Summary 44

Find Out More 45

Glossary 46

Index 48

Some words are printed in bold, **like this**. You can find out what they mean by looking in the glossary. You can also look for them in the **On The Rocks!** section at the bottom of each page.

FIERY ROCKS

Rocks have been around since Earth was formed. It takes millions of years for some rocks to form. In that time other rocks are broken down and destroyed.

Igneous rocks are the most common rocks on Earth. They are found below the ocean floor. They make up large areas of the land. There are also islands made only of igneous rock.

⇩ **This is Boar's Tusk in the state of Wyoming. It is an igneous rock formation. Boar's Tusk is about three million years old.**

Igneous rocks are made from hot liquid rock that is partly melted. This comes from deep inside Earth.

Did you know that volcanoes produce igneous rock? Sometimes hot liquid rock flows out of volcanoes. This is known as **lava**. Lava cools and hardens to form igneous rock.

Find out later...

...how ancient people used igneous rock.

...how igneous rocks are used in sport.

...where you can find this "**granite** city."

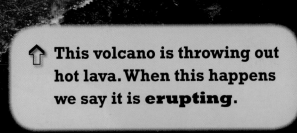

⬆ **This volcano is throwing out hot lava. When this happens we say it is erupting.**

lava name for magma (hot liquid rock) when it reaches Earth's surface

CRUSTY OLD ROCKS

What's inside Earth?

Igneous rocks begin their life inside Earth. But what is Earth like deep down?

Earth is made up of different layers. The **crust** is like its skin. There are two types of crust. They are **continental crust** and **oceanic crust**.

Continental crust is beneath the land. It is up to 43.5 miles (70 kilometers) thick.

Digging deeper
Earth's crust is made from rock. But we cannot always see this rock. This is because it may be covered with water, soil, or buildings.

⬇ This is an area in the country of Algeria. Here we can clearly see Earth's crust. We can see it is made of rock.

crust thin surface layer of Earth. It is made of rock.

Oceanic crust is beneath the oceans. It is up to 6.2 miles (10 kilometers) thick.

Under the crust is the **mantle**. This layer is 1,800 miles (2,900 kilometers) deep. Igneous rocks start their life there.

The **core** is at the center of Earth. There is a solid inner core and a liquid outer core. The inner core is made of hard metal. The outer core is melted metal.

Melting rocks
The rocks in the mantle are very hot. They are partly melted in places. The melted rock is known as **magma**.

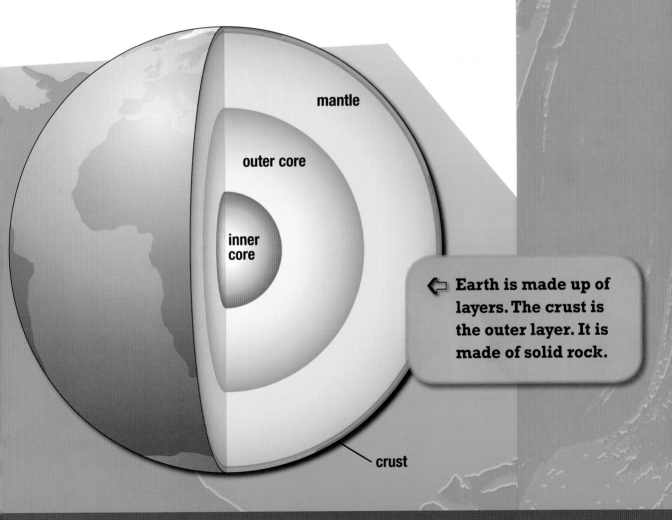

mantle

outer core

inner core

⇦ Earth is made up of layers. The crust is the outer layer. It is made of solid rock.

crust

Does the crust move?

Earth's **crust** is not one solid layer. It is broken up into huge moving pieces. These are called **plates**. They fit together like a giant jigsaw puzzle.

The plates float on the layer of Earth called the **mantle** (see page 7). They move very slowly over Earth. They move only a few inches each year. The plates carry the land and oceans with them.

In some places the plates are moving apart. This makes the crust weaker. It usually happens along

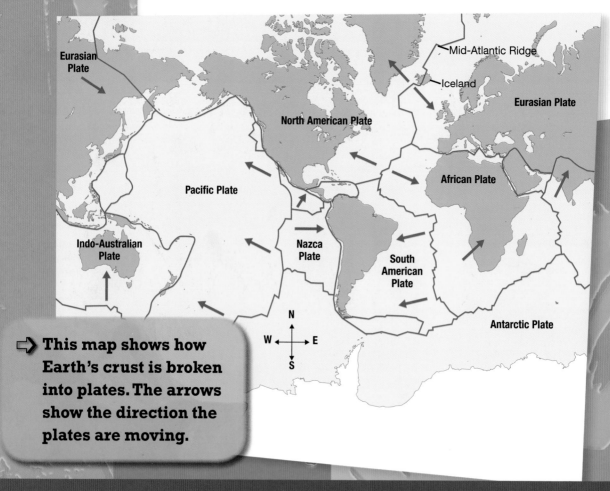

⇨ This map shows how Earth's crust is broken into plates. The arrows show the direction the plates are moving.

mountain chains on the ocean floor. Hot melted rock rises at these places. It forces its way into the crust through cracks. It forms new igneous rock.

In some places plates move toward each other. When they meet, the crust may become squashed. It may be pushed down into Earth's mantle. Huge mountains or volcanoes can form.

⇩ **This is a photo of the Andes mountain chain in South America. It has many volcanoes. They have formed where two plates meet.**

Andes mountain chain

Rocks Around the World

What are rocks?

The whole of Earth's **crust** is made of rocks. Rocks are in mountains and on the sea floor. They are in deserts and under ice. Rocks are even in gardens. But you may have to dig very deep to find them.

The rocks of Earth's crust are not all the same. There are many different types of rock.

⇓ Sometimes rocks create amazing forms. These huge columns are on the island of Skye. Skye is in the country of Scotland.

All rocks are made of **minerals**. Minerals are solid materials. They form in nature. There are more than 4,000 types of minerals on Earth. Only about 100 of these are common in rocks.

A rock may contain many different minerals. **Granite** is an igneous rock. It contains lots of quartz. Quartz is a hard mineral. This is what makes granite a hard rock.

← **You can see how different minerals make up this piece of granite rock.**

Earth's **crust** (top layer) is made up of three groups of rock:

- igneous rock
- sedimentary rock
- metamorphic rock.

These rocks form in different ways.

Igneous rocks

Igneous rocks are made from **magma**. This is hot liquid rock. It is found in Earth's **mantle** (see page 7). Magma rises up through Earth's crust. As it rises, it cools and hardens into igneous rock.

Common rocks
Granite and **basalt** are igneous rocks. Most of the **continental crust** (see page 6) is made of granite. Most of the **oceanic crust** is made of basalt.

➪ **This is hot liquid rock that has cooled to form igneous rock.**

basalt type of igneous rock formed when lava cools and solidifies

Sedimentary rocks

Sedimentary rocks are formed from bits of other rocks. Rain or wind breaks off tiny pieces of rock. Wind or rivers carry them to a new place. The bits pile up to form sedimentary rock.

Metamorphic rocks

Metamorphic rocks are rocks that have changed. Rising magma heats up the surrounding rocks. Movements in Earth's crust squash and fold rocks. This happens over millions of years. The heating and squashing changes rocks.

Rock of sand
The rock in the picture below is sandstone. This is a sedimentary rock. It forms in areas where bits of sand collect.

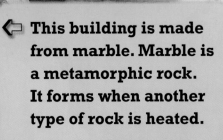

⇦ **This building is made from marble. Marble is a metamorphic rock. It forms when another type of rock is heated.**

13

The rock cycle

Rocks are formed, broken down, and formed again. This happens all the time. It is known as the **rock cycle**.

Rocks are attacked by wind and rain as soon as they appear on Earth's surface. This is known as **weathering**. Over millions of years, bits of rock are chipped off.

Oldest rocks

Earth is at least 4.5 billion years old. But there are no rocks left that are this old. The oldest rocks we know about are in the country of Canada. They are about 4 billion years old.

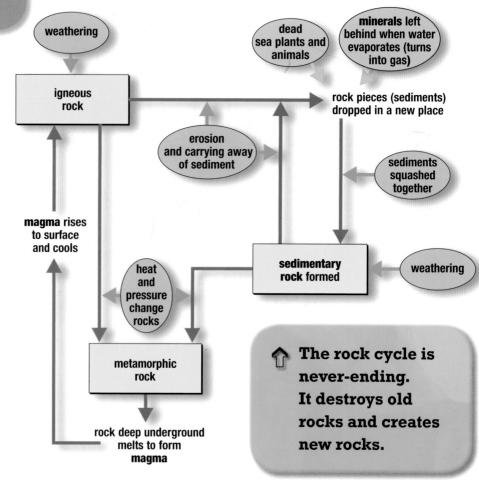

⇧ **The rock cycle is never-ending. It destroys old rocks and creates new rocks.**

Small bits of rock are carried away by wind, rivers, or ice. The removal and carrying away of rock is called **erosion**. The bits are then dropped in a new place. This process is called **deposition**.

Over millions of years, the bits of rock pile up. They are known as **sediment**. Sediment slowly changes into new rock. Then the rock cycle begins again.

In some areas Earth's **plates** (see page 8) crash into each other. The rocks there will be heated and squeezed. They change into **metamorphic rock**.

⬇ **This is one of the Devil's Marbles in the country of Australia. The Devil's Marbles are round granite boulders. Weathering has worn them down into this shape.**

WHAT MAKES IGNEOUS ROCKS?

Magma is hot liquid rock. When magma cools it becomes hard and turns into rock. Magma cools underground and at Earth's surface.

Rocks are made up of substances called **minerals**. Minerals grow as shapes. The shapes are known as **crystals**.

Igneous rocks formed underground are called **intrusive rocks**. This is because the magma intrudes (pushes into) Earth's **crust**.

Large grains

Magma cools slowly underground. There is time for large crystals (mineral parts) to form. The type of rock produced is described as **coarse grained**.

⬆ **This is coarse-grained granite rock. You can see the large mineral grains in it.**

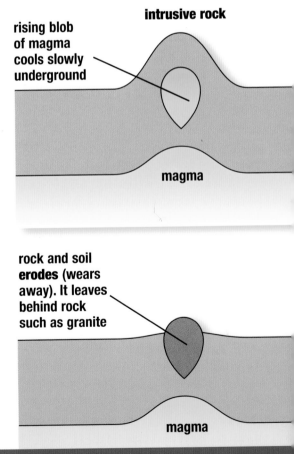

intrusive rock

rising blob of magma cools slowly underground

magma

rock and soil **erodes** (wears away). It leaves behind rock such as granite

magma

Sometimes magma rises all the way to Earth's surface. This may be on land or underwater. Then it is called **lava**. Lava can come out of volcanoes. Rocks that form on the surface are called **extrusive rocks**. This is because the magma extrudes (pushes out through) Earth's crust.

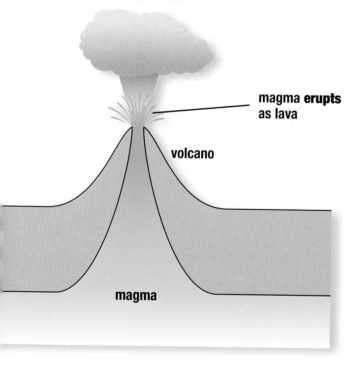

extrusive rock

magma **erupts** as lava

volcano

magma

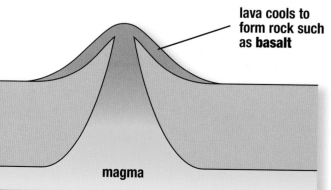

lava cools to form rock such as **basalt**

magma

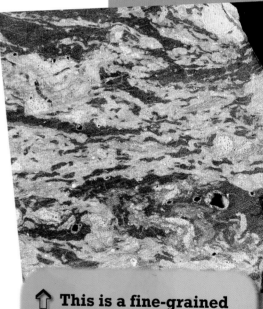

⇧ **This is a fine-grained rock called rhyolite. The mineral grains are too small to see.**

Igneous rocks can be divided into groups by:

- the size of their grains
- the **minerals** they contain
- their color
- their **texture** (what they feel like).

Grain size

Minerals grow in shapes known as **crystals.** A rock with crystals larger than 0.2 inches (5 millimeters) across is called **coarse grained**. A rock with crystals less than 0.04 inches (1 millimeter) across is **fine grained. Medium-grained** rocks have crystals between these measurements.

⇨ **This is a lump of granite. It contains the minerals quartz and feldspar. It also has small amounts of mica and hornblende.**

quartz

mineral   substance found in nature. Rocks are made from lots of minerals.

Minerals present

Igneous rocks can also be grouped according to the main minerals they contain. For example, **granite** and rhyolite can be grouped together. These rocks contain four main minerals. They are quartz, feldspar, mica, and hornblende.

feldspar

mica

hornblende

Color

Igneous rocks come in many colors. A rock is made of materials called **minerals**. Its color depends on the minerals its contains. For example, gray or black rock has lots of dark minerals.

Texture

The **texture** of a rock is how it feels. This depends on the shape of the **crystals** (mineral parts). It also depends on the size of the crystals. In some rocks the crystals are all about the same size. Others have crystals that are a mixture of sizes.

The chart on page 21 describes different rock textures.

⬇ This is an igneous rock called **obsidian**. Its grains are very fine. This makes it appear glassy.

crystal   structure within a mineral

Texture		Description	Example
phaneritic		rocks are made entirely of large crystals	**granite**
aphanitic		rocks are made entirely of small crystals	**basalt**
porphyritic		rocks are mostly made of small crystals. But they also contain a few large crystals.	**andesite**
glassy		rocks cool quickly. There is no time for crystals to form. The rocks look like glass.	**obsidian**
vesicular		rocks contain lots of holes (**vesicles**). They form when gas bubbles get trapped in **lava** (hot liquid rock).	**pumice**

vesicle gas bubble in a rock

THIS ROCK, THAT ROCK

There are many types of igneous rock. We can group igneous rocks by the main **minerals** they contain.

Granite, pegmatite, rhyolite, pumice, and obsidian rocks

The main minerals found in all these rocks are quartz and feldspar.

Granite (see pages 18–19) and pegmatite (below) are both **intrusive rocks**. This means they have

Time to grow

Pegmatite is a very coarse-grained rock. It takes millions of years to cool and harden underground. There is plenty of time for large crystals to grow.

⇩ Some pegmatite contains large, beautiful crystals. They are used in jewelry.

formed underground. Large **crystals** (mineral parts) make them **coarse grained**.

Rhyolite, **obsidian,** and pumice (see below) are all **extrusive rocks**. This means they formed on Earth's surface.

Rhyolite is usually pale gray and glassy. Its small crystals make it **fine grained**. But it often has a few large crystals, too.

No time to grow
Obsidian (see page 20) is a glassy rock. You cannot see any crystals. Obsidian cools quickly on Earth's surface. There is no time for crystals to grow.

⇦ **Pumice is full of bubblelike holes. They make pumice very light. It is the only rock that can float on water.**

Diorite and andesite

Diorite and **andesite** are igneous rocks. Feldspar is the main **mineral** in both rocks. Minerals are solid materials that make up rocks.

Diorite forms underground. This makes it an **intrusive rock**. Diorite has large **crystals** (mineral parts). It is usually speckled black and white.

Andesite forms on Earth's surface. This makes it an **extrusive rock**. Andesite has mostly small crystals. It can look glassy. Sometimes it contains **vesicles** (bubblelike holes).

Andesite Andes
Andesite rock is named for the Andes mountain chain. The Andes mountains are in South America. They are made mainly from this kind of rock.

⇩ **This volcano is called Cotopaxi. It is one of many volcanoes in the Andes mountain chain.**

Gabbro and basalt

Gabbro and **basalt** are igneous rocks. They are both made of the minerals feldspar and pyroxene. But the rocks look very different. This is because they form in different ways.

Basalt is an extrusive rock. It is black in color. It may be glassy or contain vesicles.

Gabbro is an intrusive rock. It has larger crystals than basalt. Gabbro is usually dark gray or black.

⬇ **This formation is known as Giant's Causeway. It is in Northern Ireland in the United Kingdom. The six-sided columns are made of basalt.**

How can we identify igneous rocks?

Every day you see rocks. You see them in fields. You see them in buildings. How can you tell what type of rock it is? It is not always easy to tell if a rock is igneous or not.

Look closely at the rock. Rocks are made of substances called **minerals**. Minerals grow in shapes called **crystals**. Can you see the different

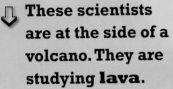

⬇ **These scientists are at the side of a volcano. They are studying lava.**

mineral   substance found in nature. Rocks are made from lots of minerals.

mineral grains? Is the rock made of up of crystals joined together? If the answers are yes, then it may be an igneous rock.

You may not see any pieces in the rock. To identify a rock like this scientists often use **microscopes**. A microscope makes things look bigger. It allows scientists to see what minerals are in the rock. Then they can identify igneous rocks that are made up of tiny crystals.

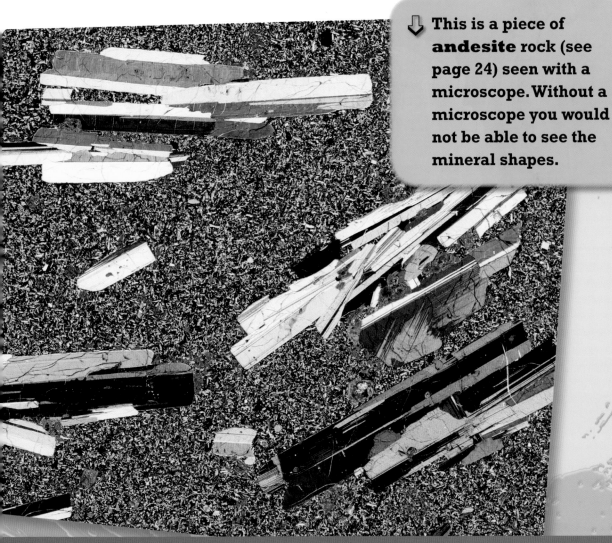

⇩ **This is a piece of andesite rock (see page 24) seen with a microscope. Without a microscope you would not be able to see the mineral shapes.**

microscope   device used to see very small objects. It makes them appear bigger.

27

BUILDINGS AND BLING

How do we use igneous rocks?

You know what igneous rocks look like. Now look out for the different ways that people use them.

Granite is a hard and **durable** rock. Durable means it is tough and lasts a long time. This is why it is used on the outside of buildings. It is also used for statues and steps.

Granite at home

Granite is both beautiful and tough. Polished granite is often used for work tops in kitchens and bathrooms.

This is the city of Aberdeen in the country of Scotland. It is known as the "granite city." This is because it has many granite buildings.

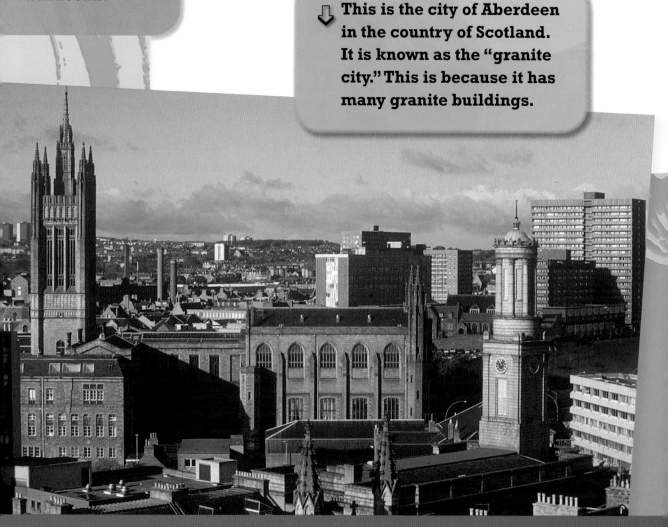

Basalt is another hard and durable rock. It is often used in parking lots and roads. This is because it can take the weight of cars driving over it.

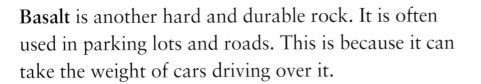

Sporting stones
Curling (pictured below) is a sport. People slide stones across ice. They try to get the stones close to a target. Curling stones are made of granite.

Obsidian has a glassy surface. It looks shiny and beautiful. Because of this, obsidian is used to make ornaments and jewelry.

Diamonds are found in an igneous rock called kimberlite. Diamond is the hardest known natural substance in the world. It is used to make cutting tools. Diamonds are also used in jewelry. They are cut in special ways to make them sparkle.

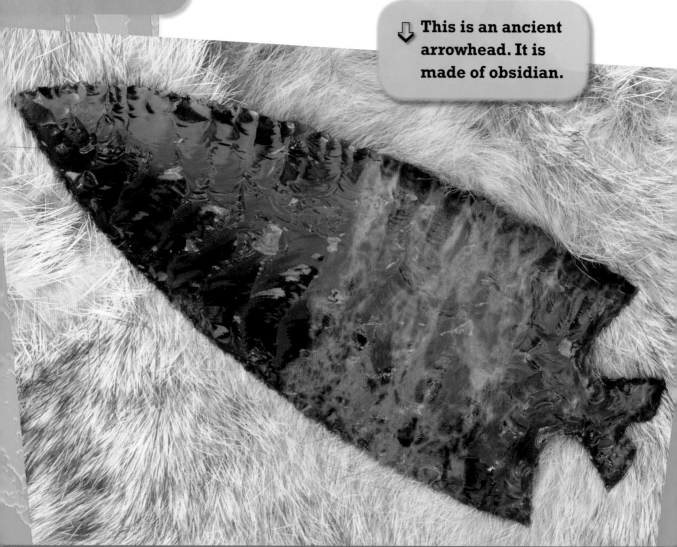

⇩ This is an ancient arrowhead. It is made of obsidian.

obsidian   extrusive igneous rock. It is jet black with a glassy appearance.

Many igneous rocks contain **metal ores**. These are mixtures of **minerals** that contain useful metals. Iron, tin, and silver are all metals. Metal ores are dug out of the ground. The metals are then separated out.

Metals are used in many ways. Gold, platinum, and copper are all metals. Gold and platinum are used for jewelry. Copper is used for pipes and wires.

Diamond drills
Did you know there are diamonds in a dentist's drill? Diamonds are so hard that they easily wear away pieces of tooth.

⬆ **This ring is made from platinum and diamond. Both the platinum and diamond are found in igneous rocks.**

INTRUSIONS

Intrusive igneous **rocks** are rocks that cool and harden underground. We can see them where soil and rocks around them have **eroded** (worn away). They are also known as **intrusions**. Intrusions have many forms.

Batholiths and tors

Magma is hot liquid rock. It rises into Earth's **crust**, or top layer. Then it cools. Sometimes it forms huge lumps of rock. These are known as **plutons**.

⇩ **This is Sugar Loaf Mountain in the country of Brazil. It is an example of a batholith.**

batholith   huge lump of intrusive granite rock that appears at Earth's surface

Enormous plutons can appear at Earth's surface. Then they are known as **batholiths**. Some cover hundreds or thousands of square miles.

In some places the batholiths themselves have been worn away. This can create forms called **tors**. Tors look like piles of boulders stacked one on top of the other.

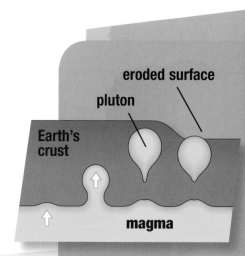

eroded surface

pluton

Earth's crust

magma

Batholiths are plutons which appear at Earth's surface. This happens when rocks above them are eroded (worn away).

⬆ This rock formation is called a tor. It is formed from **granite**.

tor   rock formation. It can form when a batholith is eroded (worn away).

Dikes, sills, and plugs

Sometimes the top of a sheet of igneous rock sticks out of the ground. This is called a **dike**. A dike usually cuts across surrounding rocks. It sticks up because it is harder than the rocks around it. It does not **erode** (wear away) as easily as they do.

A **sill** is a formation similar to a dike. But it doesn't cut across surrounding rocks. Instead it lies between other layers of rock. When sills are eroded they usually form cliffs.

The Great Dyke
The Great Dyke runs through the middle of the African country of Zimbabwe. It is 340 miles (550 kilometers) long.

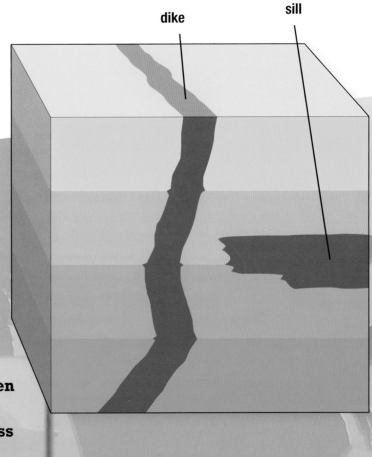

dike

sill

⇨ **A sill lies between layers of rock. A dike cuts across layers of rock.**

Hot liquid rock known as **magma** rises up through volcanoes. Sometimes the magma does not reach the surface. Instead it cools inside the volcano. It hardens into a long thin tube of rock.

Over millions of years, the softer rocks around the volcano may erode. The hard tube of rock is left behind. This is called a **volcanic plug**.

Towering rocks
The picture below shows a famous volcanic plug known as Shiprock. It is in the state of New Mexico. This huge rocky tower is more than 1,300 feet (400 meters) high.

This is Devil's Tower in the state of Wyoming. It is a volcanic plug. Rocks around it have eroded.

volcanic plug   long thin tube of igneous rock that forms
when magma cools inside a volcano

EXTRUSIONS

Saving lives
Volcanologists
are scientists who
study volcanoes.
They try to work
out when a volcano
will **erupt**. Their
work can save
many lives.

Extrusive igneous **rocks** form at Earth's surface.
These form when **magma** (hot liquid rock) reaches
the surface. They are also known as **extrusions**.

Mountains of fire

The top layer of Earth is called the **crust** (see
page 6). Volcanoes form where there is a break in
the crust. Magma rises through the break.

When magma reaches the surface, it is called **lava**.
Over millions of years, the lava builds up.

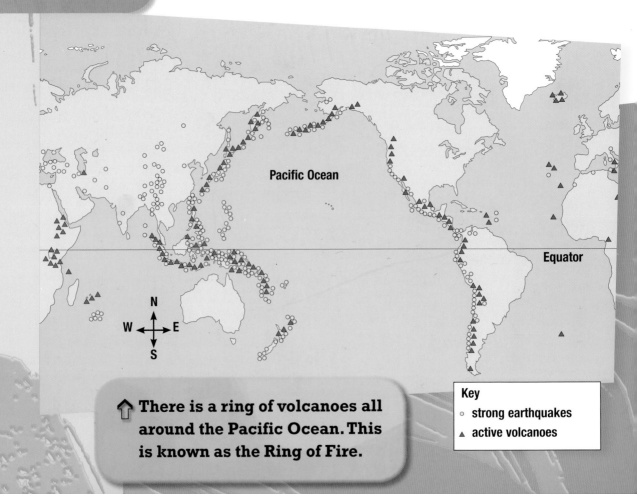

Pacific Ocean

Equator

N
W ← → E
S

⬆ There is a ring of volcanoes all
around the Pacific Ocean. This
is known as the Ring of Fire.

Key
○ strong earthquakes
▲ active volcanoes

lava   name for magma (hot liquid rock) when it reaches
Earth's surface

Lava creates the mountainlike shape of a volcano. It can produce other forms, too. The form depends on how runny the lava is.

Basalt lava is a very runny type of lava. It can spread out in huge sheets. These are called **continental flood basalts.** This is because they run over land like flood water. They have created large areas of flat land.

A flood of basalt
A continental flood basalt erupted in the country of India. This happened 65 million years ago. It covered half of India.

⇩ **This area in the country of India was formed by a massive flow of lava. It was a continental flood basalt.**

Underwater lava

There are more than 500 **active** volcanoes on Earth. Active volcanoes are ones that throw out **lava** (hot liquid rock). Most are on the ocean floor.

Plates are huge pieces of rock that make up Earth's **crust** (top layer). In some places the plates move apart. Lava flows out of the gap between them.

There is a gap in the middle of the Atlantic Ocean. Lava has built up here. It forms a long underwater mountain chain. The chain is called the Mid-Atlantic Ridge (see the map on page 8).

➡ **The country of Iceland sits on top of a huge underwater mountain chain. The chain is made of lava.**

active describes a volcano that is erupting or may erupt in the future

In one place the ridge sticks up above the water. It forms the country of Iceland.

Lava shapes

Lava can harden in different forms. Pahoehoe lava looks like a pile of ropes. A'a lava looks like the rubble you find on a building site. Pillow lava looks like lots of pillows.

⬅ **This is a pahoehoe lava flow in the state of Hawaii.**

⬆ **An a'a lava flow has formed igneous rock.**

Hot spots

We know that volcanoes form where **plates** meet. Plates are the sections of rock that make up Earth's **crust** (outer layer). But some volcanoes form in the middle of plates. How do they get there?

These volcanoes form in **hot spots.** Below Earth's crust is **magma.** This is hot liquid rock. A hot spot

⇨ **The Hawaiian Islands are slowly moving away from a hot spot. As this happens, the volcanoes become less active.**

is where the magma is unusually hot. It is so hot that it breaks through the crust. It leaks out as **lava**. Over millions of years this forms a volcano.

The Hawaiian Islands are volcanoes in the middle of a plate. They formed over a hot spot on the floor of the Pacific Ocean.

⬇ **This volcano is named Mauna Kea. It is in Hawaii. In the background you can see the world's largest volcano, called Mauna Loa.**

Largest volcano
The world's largest volcano is Mauna Loa. It is in the state of Hawaii. Mauna Loa rises over 29,528 feet (9,000 meters) from the ocean floor.

Violent volcanoes

When a volcano **erupts**, it throws out **lava** (hot liquid rock). Many volcanoes also throw out broken bits of rock. These are called **pyroclasts**. These may be fine pieces of ash. They may be rocks the size of footballs.

Sometimes a volcano erupts with great force. Then its top may blow off. This leaves a large circular dip. It is called a **crater**.

Watery volcano
Crater Lake is a lake in a volcano crater. It is in the state of Oregon. This huge lake is 1,970 feet (600 meters) deep.

⇩ This ash and rock comes from Mount Pinatubo in the Philippines. It erupted in June 1991.

An erupting volcano can cause many deaths. In 1985 the Nevado del Ruiz volcano in the country of Colombia erupted. It was a small eruption. But 23,000 people died.

The eruption caused mud to slide down the mountain. Nearby towns and villages were buried in mud. This is why many people died.

Deadly volcanoes

The following are three of the world's most deadly volcanic eruptions.

Year	Volcano	Location	Deaths
1815	Tambora	Indonesia	92,000
1883	Krakatoa	Indonesia	36,000
1902	Pelée	Martinique	28,000

⬇ **This crater is in the country of El Salvador. It formed when an eruption blew the top off the volcano.**

crater

SUMMARY

- Igneous rocks are everywhere. They are found below oceans. They are also on the land around us.

- Igneous rocks begin as **magma**. This is hot liquid rock from inside Earth. Over millions of years, magma rises up into Earth's **crust** (top layer). Sometimes it explodes out of volcanoes. Then it hardens into igneous rock.

- Igneous rocks can take many forms. They may be flat sheets of rock. They may be lumps the size of mountains.

- Some igneous rocks form at Earth's surface. These are usually made of small grains.

- Other rocks form underground. These have larger grains.

- In the past people used igneous rocks in tools, weapons, and jewels. They are still used for all kinds of things. They are used in buildings, bracelets, and bathrooms.

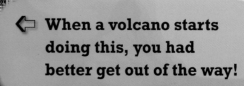

← **When a volcano starts doing this, you had better get out of the way!**

FIND OUT MORE

Books

Green, Jen. *Geology* (Routes of Science). Farmington Hills, MI: Blackbirch Press, 2004.

Harman, Rebecca. *Earth's Processes: Rock Cycles.* Chicago: Heinemann, 2005.

Slade, Suzanne. *The Rock Cycle.* New York: Rosen, 2007.

Steele, Christy. *Volcanoes* (Nature on the Rampage). Chicago: Raintree, 2003.

Symes, R. F. *Rocks & Minerals* (DK Eyewitness Books). New York: DK, 2004.

Using the Internet

If you want to find out more about igneous rock you can search the Internet. Try using keywords such as these:

- batholith
- magma
- pluton.

You can also use different keywords. Try choosing some words from this book.

Try using a search directory, such as www.yahooligans.com

Search tips

There are billions of pages on the Internet. It can be difficult to find what you are looking for. These search skills will help you find useful websites more quickly:

- Know exactly what you want to find out about.
- Use two to six keywords in a search. Put the most important words first.
- Only use names of people, places, or things.

Glossary

accessory mineral mineral found in a rock in tiny quantities

active describes a volcano that is erupting or may erupt in the future

andesite fine-grained, extrusive igneous rock

basalt type of igneous rock formed when lava cools and solidifies

batholith huge lump of intrusive granite rock that appears at Earth's surface

coarse grained large grains

continental crust parts of Earth's crust that lie beneath the land

continental flood basalt huge sheet of basalt lava

core center of Earth

crater circular dip at the top of a volcano

crust thin surface layer of Earth. It is made of rock.

crystal structure within a mineral

deposition laying down weathered rock in a new place

dike vertical sheet of igneous rock that cuts across layers of rock

durable able to stand up to weathering

erode wear away and remove

erosion wearing away and removal of rock

erupt to throw out lava and ash

extrusion body of igneous rock that forms at Earth's surface

extrusive rock igneous rock that forms on the surface of Earth

fine grained tiny grains that you need a microscope to see

granite coarse-grained, extrusive igneous rock

hot spot area where the mantle is particularly hot

intrusion body of igneous rock that forms underground

intrusive rock igneous rock that forms underground

lava name for magma (hot liquid rock) when it reaches Earth's surface

magma hot melted rock from inside Earth

mantle hot layer of Earth beneath the crust

medium grained grains between 0.02 inches (5 millimeters) and 0.4 inches (1 millimeter) across

metal ore mixture of minerals that contain useful metals

metamorphic rock rock formed when igneous or sedimentary rocks are changed by heat or pressure

microscope device used to see very small objects. It makes them appear bigger.

mineral substance found in nature. Rocks are made from lots of minerals.

obsidian extrusive igneous rock. It is jet black with a glassy appearance.

oceanic crust parts of Earth's crust that lie beneath the oceans

plate giant, moving piece of Earth's crust

pluton huge domed lump of intrusive rock underground

pyroclast rock thrown out of a volcano when it erupts

rock cycle unending cycle of rock formation and destruction

sediment pieces of rock that have been worn away and moved to another place

sedimentary rock rock formed from the broken pieces of other rocks

sill sheet of igneous rock that lies between layers of rocks

texture how something feels

tor rock formation. It can form when a batholith is eroded (worn away).

vesicle gas bubble in a rock

volcanic plug long thin tube of igneous rock that forms when magma cools inside a volcano

weathering breaking down of rock by the weather

INDEX

accessory minerals 19
andesite 21, 24, 27

basalt 12, 21, 25, 29, 37
batholiths 32–33

coarse-grained rocks 16, 18, 44
colors 20
continental crust 6, 12
continental flood basalts 37
copper 31
craters 42, 43
crystals 16, 17, 18, 20, 22, 23, 26, 27

deposition 15
diamonds 30, 31
dikes 34
diorite 24

Earth's core 7
Earth's crust 6, 7, 8, 10, 12, 13, 16, 40, 44
erosion 15, 32, 33, 34, 35
extrusive rocks 17, 23, 24, 25, 36

feldspar 18, 19, 22, 24, 25
fine-grained rocks 17, 18, 20, 23, 44

gabbro 25
gold 31
grain size 18, 20, 21
granite 11, 12, 16, 18–19, 21, 22,
    28–29
grouping igneous rocks 18–21, 22–25

hornblende 18, 19
hot spots 40–41

intrusive rocks 16, 22–23, 24, 25, 32
iron 31

kimberlite 30

lava 5, 17, 21, 36–39, 41, 42

magma 7, 12, 13, 16–17, 32, 35, 40–41, 44
mantle 7, 8, 9, 12
marble 13
medium-grained rocks 18
metal ores 31
metamorphic rock 12, 13, 15
mica 18, 19
Mid-Atlantic Ridge 8, 38–39
minerals 11, 16, 19, 20, 22, 26–27, 31
mountain formation 9, 38

obsidian 20, 21, 23, 30
oceanic crust 6, 12

pegmatite 22
plates 8–9, 15, 38, 40, 41
platinum 31
plutons 32, 33
pumice 21, 23
pyroclasts 42
pyroxene 25

quartz 11, 18, 19, 22

rhyolite 17, 19, 23
rock cycle 14–15
rock formation 12–15, 16–17

sandstone 13
sedimentary rock 12, 13, 14
sills 34
silver 31

textures 18, 20, 21
tin 31
tors 32, 33

uses of rocks 28–31

vesicles 21, 23, 24, 25
volcanic plugs 35
volcanoes 5, 9, 17, 24, 36–38, 40–43

weathering 14, 15